Poem-maker, Word-shaker

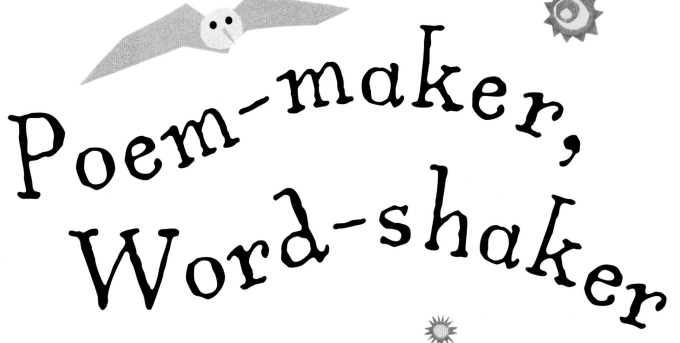

Pie Corbett

Chrysalis Children's Books

First published in the UK in 2005 by
Chrysalis Children's Books
An imprint of Chrysalis Books Group Plc
The Chrysalis Building, Bramley Road
London W10 6SP

ISBN 1 84458 188 8

British Library Cataloguing in Publication
Data for this book is available from the
British Library.

Associate publisher: Joyce Bentley
Editor and project manager: Nicola Edwards
Designers: Rachel Hamdi, Holly Mann
Illustrators: Andrew Breakspeare,
Abigail Conway, Serena Curmi, Sarah Fisher,
Emma Garner, Sarah Garson,
Maddy McClellan, Kate Pankhurst.

Printed in China

10 9 8 7 6 5 4 3 2 1

Contents

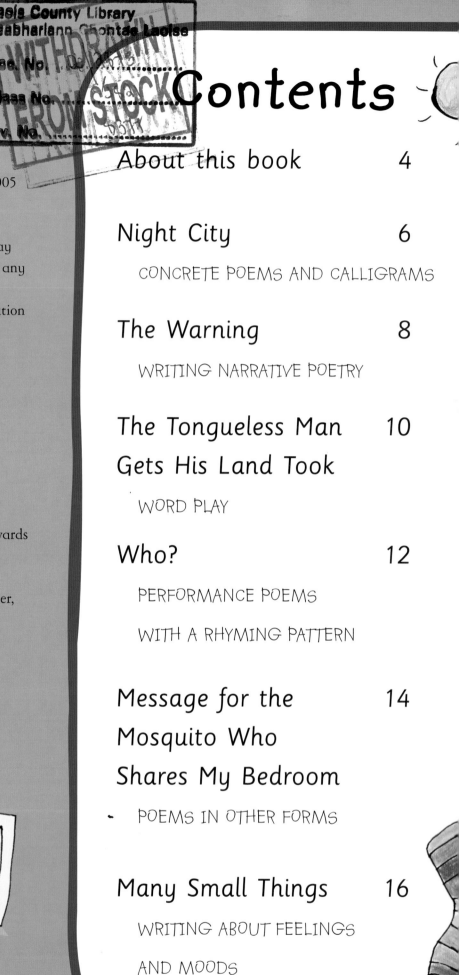

About this book

"**Hello**. My name is Pie Corbett (yes, I know – silly name, isn't it?). If, like me, you enjoy writing poetry – or even if you think you don't – then this is the book for you! In it you will find lots of ideas and examples to help you with your writing. You won't need much else – just a pencil, a notebook and plenty of imagination. Everyone dreams, everyone wonders 'what would happen if….' – and that is using your imagination!

Some of the poems in this book are all about looking closely at the world around you and being aware of your senses.

I'll show you how you can use a few poetic techniques to capture forever what you saw and how you felt.

Several of the poems are more about playing with ideas and words. Some have a form to follow – a repeating pattern or a rhyming pattern. For each type of poem I'll give you an example and then show you step by step how you can write your own version. If you find this hard at first, do not worry – your writing will get better with practice. Just write what you want to write, then read back through your poem. Check that you've chosen the best words to help your poem say what you really want it to say."

How to use the book

A poem I've written or one I remember from when I was at school

Poem technique featured

My ideas about the poem

A step-by-step guide to writing your own poem

What Am I?

If you stare at me,
I will not blush.
I cannot lie.

Like an eye,
I am a porthole on your world.
Even when you ignore me
I cannot help pursuing
Every move you take –
Real, yet a fake,
I wait, watching whatever happens,
Making no judgements.

I am too honest for most
And can only boast the truth.
You search my soul for beauty
And I throw back your twin.

Silent, silver and as still
As a perfect lake, dawn fills me up;
Greedy night leaves me empty.

I hold everything and yet my cupboard is bare.

Dare to smash me,
And I'll bring seven years
Of ill fortune
To bless your home.

About this poem

"We use riddles all the time when we speak. For instance, if someone says 'it's raining cats and dogs', that is a sort of riddle – you have to work out the meaning behind the words. Did you guess that my poem was about a mirror?"

Over to you

Now write a riddle of your own. First, think of a subject, e.g. an eye. Then make a list of all sorts of things to do with your subject – ask yourself what it does (looks, stares, glares), who uses it (creatures, needle, storm), colours (blue, brown, green), shape (round), size (small), any sounds it makes (silent), expressions about it (keeping an eye on things) and so on.

To write the poem, pretend the object is speaking. Start with the words 'I am….'. Drop in clues but do not give it away! Use similes to compare your subject to other things, to build a picture in your readers' minds.

I am silent,
Peering at the world.
Small as a marble.

Writing tip

In the poem I also use metaphors. Metaphors are very like similes. But instead of saying that one thing is like another, you say that one thing has become another, e.g. **I am a porthole on your world.** When I write 'greedy night' that also is a metaphor because I have made it sound as if the night was alive like some sort of monster!

More ideas

Other good subjects for riddles include a lock and key, a pond, a raindrop, a snake, a star, a cloud and a tree.

Riddles using similes and metaphors

More ideas for creating similar types of poem

Tips to help you with writing or performing your poems

Use the chart on page 5 to find out about the poems included in the book and the poetic techniques they feature. The chart also lists well-known examples of the same types of poem.

Poem	Type	Features	Other examples
Night City	Concrete poem Calligram	Words used to make shapes. Letters written to reflect meaning.	The Tail – Lewis Carroll
The Warning	Narrative poem	Free verse	Chocolate Cake – Michael Rosen
The Tongueless Man Gets His Land Took	Nonsense poem	Idiom Word play Alliteration	hist whist – e.e. cummings
Who?	Performance poem Rhyming verse	Rhyme Repetition Senses	Who Killed Cock Robin? – anon.
Message for the Mosquito Who Shares My Bedroom	Free verse Monologue	Word play	Knoxville, Tennesse – Nikki Giovanni
Many Small Things	Poem about feelings and moods	List Pattern Alliteration	A Poison Tree – William Blake
What Am I?	Riddle Monologue	Similes Metaphors	You're – Sylvia Plath
City Dawn	Free verse	Personification Alliteration Metaphors	The Sea – James Reeves
Poem for Tamzin	List poem	Senses Observation Alliteration Similes	The Magic Box – Kit Wright
Day-sleeper, Night-stalker	Kenning Monologue Riddle	Metaphors Rhyme	Penguin – Sue Cowling
Haiku Seasons	Poems in a sequence Haiku Tanka Cinquain	Seasons Senses Observation Syllables	Haiku - Basho
The Woodsprite Speaks	Monologue	Senses Different viewpoint	Stopping by Woods on a Snowy Evening – Robert Frost

Night City

Silvery scythe slicing the dark.

I wait at night, tall as a mast.

Weaving the blue.

Like a goldfish bowl - stare in. As we glare out.

I am the mouth of the house.

Purring by, ignoring the streets.

crept along the wall and jumped off.

The cat leapt,

About this poem

❝ Words are like plastic – you can mould them into shapes and use them to create word-pictures. ❞

Over to you

To make a concrete poem, first you need to choose a subject to write about. Then draw a thin outline of the subject. If you were writing about the sun, it might look like the drawing on the right.

Then decide what you want to write about your subject and arrange the words so that they follow the shape.

Good subjects for concrete poems include a face, the moon, rain, a tree, a lollipop, and a television.

The daily helter-skelter of summery swelter.

Calligrams

You can make a calligram by changing the way in which a word is written so that the shape reflects the meaning.

THIN "SHIVER" FAT

Try making calligrams with the words shake, tall, small, curled and ball. Add ideas of your own, too.

More ideas

Another way to make a calligram is by writing a sentence and then setting it out so that the letter shapes and pattern reflect the meaning. Look back at the leaping, creeping cat calligram on p6. You could make calligrams about a slithering snake, a weeping willow or a rocky avalanche.

The Warning

My mother
Had warned me often enough –

But I took no notice
Of that sort of stuff –

As soon as her back was turned
I burned off,
Out over the back wall
And down town.

Where I mucked about
With the free-range eggs.

For a dare, it was –
Yes, there it was – high up
On the town hall wall.
So small and frail,
Yet up I climbed
As the town clock chimed.

Showing off to the world,
I sat there, legs dangling,
Laughing into the wind –
And the town far below
Like a miniature world.

For a moment, I was the King
The new 'big thing'.

Till I felt a sudden jolt
And I was hurled down,
Tumbling till I landed like Jack;
Broke my crown,
Cracked my back.

"Listen," I whispered,
"I was pushed!"

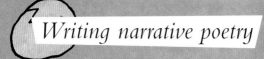

About this poem

 In this poem I took a well-known rhyme and pretended that I was the main character. Did you guess I was Humpty Dumpty? When you write a poem you can be whoever you want! **99**

Over to you

You could use a nursery rhyme, a traditional tale, a fable, a myth or a legend as a source for a retelling.

It makes your poem more interesting if you take a new angle. For instance you could write as if you were one of the characters. Which character from a traditional story do you think is speaking in this poem?

I'm fed up
With Jack –
I sent him out yesterday
To take the cow now,
Down to the market.
We needed a good price –
And what do you think
He came home with –
A handful of beans!

I was not best pleased!

It can also add to the effect if you reset the story in modern times. Whose story has been updated here?

Yesterday my Mum asked me
To take some shopping over
to My Gran's
On the other side of the estate...

The answers are at the bottom of the page!

 **Writing tip**

✿ Before writing the poem, tell someone your tale in role as the character. When you write, leave line breaks to help the reader – avoid lines that are too long and difficult to read. As you write keep reading the poem aloud and listen to hear if it flows and sounds easy to understand. It should sound like someone talking about what has happened to them.

Answers: The speaker is Jack's mum from Jack and the Beanstalk. Red Riding Hood's story has been updated.

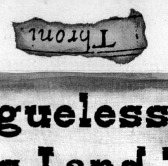

The Tongueless Man
Gets His Land Took

In England they say –
The tongueless man gets
his land took.

In Iceland they say –
The hopeless frost gets
its bravery melted.

In France they say –
The worthless baguette
gets its thorns burned.

In America they say –
The sunless bison gets its
hands shaken.

In Zanzibar they say –
The truthless wreck get
its beard burned.

In New Zealand they say –
The speechless mountain
gets its heart sung.

In space they say –
The thoughtless poem
gets its end soon.

About this poem

" I got the idea for this poem from an old saying from Cornwall in England, 'the tongueless man gets his land took'. It means that if you are not good with words then people will be able to win you over easily. I wondered what sort of sayings might come from other parts of the world. "

Over to you

You could make your own poem of silly sayings.
Use my first line:

> The tongueless man gets his land took.

Then think of a different 'less' word instead of 'tongueless', e.g. thoughtless.

Now add in a creature or object instead of the word 'man', e.g. apple, and then finish the sentence:

> The thoughtless apple gets its light switched on.

What you are doing is emptying the sentence of the words and filling it up again with new ones.

More ideas

There are many other ways to play with words. You could take everyday expressions literally:

Dad said, it was raining cats and dogs – outside we could just hear the darkness purring and the moon barking!

Write tongue twisters about your friends. Turn this into a poem by writing a whole list – perhaps for your class.

Curious Kyle camped carefully by the cold canal.
Doubtful Daisy dragged a dirty donut delightfully.

Write a sentence and then swap words around, e.g.

I kissed mum goodbye and hurried to the bus stop.

I hurried mum goodbye and kissed the bus stop.

Who?

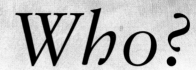

Who tasted sleep,
While the west wind blew?
I, said the son,
It was all that I knew.

Who heard the leaves
Stumble in the trees?
I, said the finch,
As they took to the breeze.

Who touched the stars;
Like pinpricks of light?
I, said the fox,
In the dark of the night.

Who smelt the frost
As it freckled the trees?
I, said the grass,
As it speckled the leaves.

Who saw the moon
Like an eye drifting by?
I, said the owl,
Saw it glide way up high.

Then who saw her leave,
With no word of warning?
I, said the dark,
As daylight was dawning.

About this poem

❝ I got the idea for my poem from a very old song, which begins like this:

> Who killed Cock Robin?
> I, said the Sparrow,
> With my bow and arrow,
> I killed Cock Robin.

I had to work hard to make sure that the verses flowed and did not sound clumsy. I wanted this poem to sound like a song. If I could sing and play an instrument I would set it to music. It would make a good performance poem. ❞

Over to you

You could write your own version of the song. First, ask a creature a question. Choose a verb to replace 'killed', e.g.

   Who heard the cat

Now add on a second line that says what the cat was doing, e.g.

   As it crept through the grass?

The third line needs to answer the question, e.g.

   I, said the dog,

Notice how our second line has six syllables in it – six beats. Your last line will need to sound the same and share the same rhyme or near rhyme at the end, e.g.

   I saw the cat slip past.

Writing tip

✪ Notice how I used the five senses to describe what the creatures in the poem tasted, touched, smelt, heard and saw. But the last verse I have left as a mystery.

Performing tip

✪ Try performing the poem in pairs or as a group. Vary the way in which you speak the verses – loud/soft, fast/slow. Use plenty of expression.

Message for the Mosquito Who Shares My Bedroom

I'M FED UP
WITH THE WAY
YOU KEEP ME AWAKE.

You wait
Till I've just turned the light off
And settled down
For a good night's zzzzzzZZZZZZZZZZZZZZ
Before starting up
Your irritating whine.
Announcing,
"Mister mosquito
is out for a bite."
At any second
I expect to feel you
Puncture my skin
And suck my blood.
Tiny vampire,
I am not your personal
Ketchup bottle.
If I find you've settled nearby,
I'll swat you flat.
Be warned —
Go pester
Some other sauce
Of blood.

About this poem

" I like trying to write poems in other forms, such as messages or diary entries, letters or posters. Last summer I wrote this poem as a message for a very irritating mosquito that kept pestering me at night. I propped up the poem at the end of my bed as a warning to leave me alone! "

Over to you

You could write messages for anyone or anything you like – traffic jams, arguments, clouds, flames, tables, giggles…Think carefully about how the subject of your message makes you feel.

Try writing poems as notes, lists, diary entries or letters. Make them inventive – you could pretend to be an animal or a character from a traditional tale or nursery rhyme.

Think about how your character would feel about what happens to them. For example, a diary entry from one of the three little pigs might begin like this:

Woke early this morning to
a terrible gale.
The straw walls shuddered…

Look for any places where you could improve your poem.
Cut out unnecessary words, e.g.

Cat – I felt tired,
weary and exhausted
So I went for a nap… could become:

Cat – I felt tired,
So I went for a nap…

Writing tip

✧ Notice how at the end of my poem. I use the word 'sauce', which sounds the same as 'source'. This is called a play on words because of the two meanings:

• Sauce – a liquid like tomato ketchup (the blood);

• Source – the place from which something comes (the source of food for the mosquito).

Many Small Things

There are many small things
that give me pleasure —

The sun slapping me
first thing in the morning when I step outside.

Arriving at the bus stop
just as the number eleven pulls up
so that I don't have to queue.

Sniffing the pages of a new book,
popping the bubbles on bubble-wrap,
clicking my biro top,
and tugging the Velcro tongue
on my trainers,

Being able to click my fingers
and crack my knuckles.

Making my eyes cross
and meet in the middle.

Getting away with wearing
the same pair of socks for over a week.

Yes, there are many small things
that give me delight.

About this poem

" I spent some time thinking about all sorts of little, everyday things I used to enjoy when I was at school. They were things that came for free with no effort rather than big things like holidays or birthdays. I then turned them into this list poem. "

Over to you

There are many different ways to write about your feelings and moods. You could write the same sort of list as mine, or make up another title for a different mood or feeling:

- Peaceful things
- Things that make me angry
- Silly things
- Special things

- Sad things
- Funny things
- Irritating things

First, make a list of ideas – peaceful things might include snow falling, grass growing and stones in the sun.

Next write down an opening, e.g.

I like peaceful things –

Then turn each idea into a short line, e.g.

I like peaceful things –
Snow falling on hard earth,
Grass growing in the spring,
Stones warming themselves in the sun...

Writing tip

☆ Notice how every now and then I put words close together that start with the same sound:

sun slapping

tugging... tongue

This is called alliteration. It is a useful technique because it makes the words more memorable.

What Am I?

If you stare at me,
I will not blush.
I cannot lie.

Like an eye,
I am a porthole on your world.
Even when you ignore me
I cannot help pursuing
Every move you take –
Real, yet a fake,
I wait, watching whatever happens,
Making no judgements.

I am too honest for most
And can only boast the truth.
You search my soul for beauty
And I throw back your twin.

Silent, silver and as still
As a perfect lake, dawn fills me up;
Greedy night leaves me empty.

I hold everything and yet my cupboard is bare.

Dare to smash me,
And I'll bring seven years
Of ill fortune
To bless your home.

About this poem

"We use riddles all the time when we speak. For instance, if someone says 'it's raining cats and dogs', that is a sort of riddle – you have to work out the meaning behind the words. Did you guess that my poem was about a mirror?"

Over to you

Now write a riddle of your own. First, think of a subject, e.g. *an eye*. Then make a list of all sorts of things to do with your subject – ask yourself what it does (*looks, stares, glares*), who uses it (*creatures, needle, storm*), colours (*blue, brown, green*), shape (*round*), size (*small*), any sounds it makes (*silent*), expressions about it (*keeping an eye on things*) and so on.

To write the poem, pretend the object is speaking. Start with the words 'I am…'. Drop in clues but do not give it away! Use similes to compare your subject to other things, to build a picture in your readers' minds.

I am silent,
Peering at the world.
Small as a marble...

Writing tip

✦ In the poem I also use metaphors. Metaphors are very like similes. But instead of saying that one thing is *like* another, you say that one thing has *become* another, e.g.

I am a porthole on your world.

When I write 'greedy night' that also is a metaphor because I have made it sound as if the night was alive like some sort of monster!

More ideas

Other good subjects for riddles include a lock and key, a pond, a raindrop, a snake, a star, a cloud and a tree.

City Dawn

Restless streets yawn;
Dawn creeps in.

Newspapers tussle in the gutter;
Early buses mutter
Down the street.

From the subway —
Office workers blink
Into white daylight,
A silent stream flowing
Down the road.

Taxis wait —
Like fat toads.

A traffic light blinks
Its red eye
But no one cares.

The sun's albino stare
Lightens the tight streets.

Doorways open their mouths;
Windows peer out.

The morning grips the city.

About this poem

❝ My poem is about the city waking up in the morning. I tried to make it sound as if the city itself was alive. ❞

Over to you

To write a poem like mine, think of a place that you know well. First, make a list down the page of the things that you can see, e.g.

Newspapers   Buses

Then add a little more to each idea, putting words either side, e.g.

Newspapers tussle in the gutter;
Early buses mutter
Down the street.

Notice how I made all the 'things' sound as if they were alive. This is called personification and it is a form of metaphor. It is great fun to use this in writing, especially as it helps to create atmosphere.

Practise using personification by making a list of a few things that you can see around you. For instance, I can see – a window, a book, a computer screen.

Now pretend that the objects have come alive as if they were characters in a cartoon. What are they doing?

The window winked its eye at me.
The book slithered onto the floor.
The computer screen grinned maliciously.

Writing tip

✭ You could try using some alliteration in your poetry, e.g. 'silent stream'.

Can you find places where the words in my poem rhyme? Notice that the rhymes are not always at the ends of lines and they all make sense. Only use rhyming words if they improve the sound of your poem and help you get the meaning across to your readers.

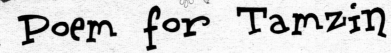

Poem for Tamzin

Your neck of the woods was mine —
Where the whale-backed hills rolled green,
Where the busy spring buds burst,
Where May blossom speckled the hedgerows,
Where the hawk hung high,
Where the skylark dizzied itself in the blue spring air
And violets dotted downland paths.

Where the sun shimmered on tarmac,
Where the swallows dived in blue like tiny anchors,
Where clouds drifted by,
Where the trout flickered silver,
Where the dragonfly hovered,
Where the hedges smelled of thyme
And at night the moon hung like a bear's claw.

Where the winds shivered through the corn,
Where the leaves fell like a deck of cards,
Where chestnuts blossomed like tiny, green bombs,
Where apples blushed and raspberries fattened,
Where lightning crackled an electric vein,
Where lanterns lit in Halloween windows
And pumpkins glowed like moons.

Where snow camouflaged the stone walls,
Where the sheep's wool froze on the barbed wire fence,
Where puddles froze and the hills crouched,
Where the stars glittered and the fields turned to steel.

Yes, your neck of the woods was mine
When I was younger
And the world was so strong
That I could taste each day.

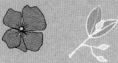

About this poem

> This is part of a poem I wrote for a girl called
> Tamzin who had won a prize – and the prize
> was a poem especially written for the winner
> by me. I noticed that Tamzin lived in the same
> area as I had been brought up in, so I wrote
> down a list of memories from my childhood.

Over to you

Try writing a list poem about where you live. To give the
list a pattern, make a verse for each season. Like me, you
could use the word 'where' to help you write the ideas.
If you live in a city you might begin winter like this:

Where the icicles hang like transparent teeth,
Where the roads turn to slush,
Where the bushes breathe frost,
Where the buses skid...

Remember that for each season you
will need to show how the city changes.
So in summer, you might mention:

Where the roads shimmer in the heat,
Where ice creams melt,
Where cats nap and dogs doze,
Where the sun idles and shadows
sidle behind...

Writing tip

✦ Experiment with using poetic
techniques such as alliteration ('dotted
downland') and similes ('like a deck of
cards') in your seasonal poem.

Choose words with care. Use:

Precise nouns – 'violets' not 'flowers'

Powerful verbs – 'shivered' not 'went'

Powerful adjectives – 'busy' buds.

Day-sleeper, Night-stalker

Leg-brusher,
Mouse-trapper,
Flea-house,
Milk-lapper!

Night-stalker,
Purr-maker,
Fur-licker,
Cheese-taker!

Day-sleeper,
Fly-catcher.
Mini-tiger,
Bird-snatcher!

About this poem

" My poem is a collection of riddles called kennings. The Vikings used kennings – they named a sword a back-biter and the sea their 'whale-road'.

A kenning is a form of metaphor because it turns one thing into another. It is also a sort of riddle because the writer keeps the real object hidden by disguising it with words. "

Over to you

To write your own kennings, first think of a subject. Choose something that you know a lot about. Make a list of all sorts of things to do with your subject. For instance, cats drink milk, catch mice, sleep a lot, hunt at night and so on.

Now you have to turn your ideas into kennings. Make up a description by using two words linked by a hyphen. For example, a cat catches mice so it becomes a mouse-trapper. A horse that eats hay becomes a hay-muncher. You could write a kenning about your teacher, e.g.

Noise-quencher,
Work-giver,
Fast-ticker,
Loud-shouter...

More ideas

You could make a collection of modern kennings, e.g.

number-cruncher (calculator)
couch-potato (lazy person)
book-worm (keen reader)
chatter-box (talkative person)

Try writing a short poem in which you take one of these kennings literally, e.g.

The box opened its lid,
Bared its teeth,
Wagged its tongue
And chattered on....

Haiku Seasons

Wintry night.
Stars pin up the sky.
Carols drift down the street.

Spring dawn.
Daffodils shake yellow skirts.
The cat purrs in sunlight.

Summer afternoon.
Heat sleeps in the back yard.
Barbecues sizzle.

Autumn dusk.
Brittle leaves stumble.
A distant dog barks.

About this poem

" Haiku are small poems that originated in Japan. They tend to be about nature, though not always. Writing a haiku is rather like taking a quick snapshot with a camera – a word snapshot of a special moment in time. "

Over to you

In Japanese, the traditional haiku is always three lines long with five syllables in the first line, seven in the second and five in the last. In English this is not necessary, though you should be able to say your haiku in one go, with one breath.

You could use my haiku as a model. Start by thinking of a season and time of day. Then imagine a typical scene – what can you see and hear? To write the haiku, follow this pattern:

Line 1 Season and time of day:
　　　Wintry night.

Line 2 Something you can see:
　　　Stars pin up the sky.

Line 3 Something you can hear:
　　　Carols drift down the street.

More ideas

Change a haiku into a tanka by adding a fourth line of seven syllables. You could write one with a friend. You each write a haiku and swap them over. Then you each write a final line of seven syllables.

Wintry night.
Stars pin up the sky.
Carols drift down the street.
Shoppers hurry past with gifts.

A cinquain uses a different pattern of 5 lines arranged as 2, 4, 6, 8 and 2 syllables. Try writing a cinquain about a scene, thinking about what you can hear.

Lis-ten – (2)
The win-ter thaw (4)
Leaves i-ci-cles dripp-ing, (6)
And the child-ren's snow-man melt-ing. (8)
Un-seen. (2)

The Woodsprite Speaks

I saw the sun creep up
And hid in an acorn's cup.

I heard the night bat squeak
And clung to its furry back.

I tasted the blackberry's juice
And blood-stained my hands.

I smelt the sharp tang of the fox
And ducked under the oak's rough skin.

I felt the stoat's smooth coat
And wore it as a cloak.

I brushed the briar's sharp thorn
And stole it for a knife.

Last thing at night
I curled tight
In a snail's shell
And dreamed
Of moon-shine.

About this poem

" I like writing poems in which I pretend to be someone else. For this poem, I imagined what it would be like to be a tiny woodsprite. The world would be a very different place! I thought hard about what it would be like to be very small and able to fly. I used the ideas to write my monologue, a poem for one speaker. "

Over to you

If you look carefully you will see that my poem begins with the dawn and ends with night-time. I run through each of the senses, describing what I could see, hear, taste, smell and touch. You could use these patterns to help you write your ideas.

Choose a creature you want to become in your poem. Imagine a day in its life. Think about how it would use its senses to experience the world around it.

Write your first line:

I saw a caterpillar crawl

Then add on an idea:

I saw a caterpillar crawl
And hitched a ride on its back.

In each couplet (pair of lines), try to use one technique, such as alliteration, adding powerful verbs or introducing a surprising idea.

Writing tip

☆ I find it helps to reread my writing and see if there are any places where I could polish it a little. For instance:

I saw the sun
and got under a stone.

Now that sounds dull, but to make it more interesting I could use a powerful verb and add in some description:

I saw the sun bristle in the air
And squeezed tight beneath a wet stone.

A Poet's Toolkit
Creating patterns and special effects

🔩 How to set your poem out

There are many different ways to set out your poems.
You could:

✧ Make a shape with the words or letters, e.g.

Weaving the blue.

✧ Use verses and choruses like a song.

✧ Use a repeating phrase to make a list:

The dreamer saw a stone on fire.
The dreamer saw a midnight choir....

✧ Count words:

In this poem
Each line will
Thrill to three...

✧ Use syllables:

Writing a haiku
is harder if you have to
count the syllables.

✧ Use a rhyming pattern:

The captain's in the cave
The hero's being brave...

✧ Make your own pattern with the words (this is called free verse):

the whisper
          of the bullets
caught
          on the barbed wire....

🔩 Two things that you can do in a poem

1. You can play with ideas:

I curled tight in a snail's shell.

2. You can also try to say what something is really like:

Silent, silver and as still
As a perfect lake...

How to use special effects

Poets use all sorts of techniques to make their writing effective.

- Use well-chosen words to build meaning in your poems, e.g.

powerful verbs	'limped' not 'came'
precise nouns	'Mercedes' not 'car'
expressive adjectives	'shy giant' not 'big giant'

- Use new and surprising
  combinations of words, e.g.   The cockrel lava poured...

- Use alliteration, e.g.   The busy bees buzzed...

- Use rhymes and rhythm, e.g.   The quick, slick clown
  wore a sorry frown.

- Use techniques to build a clear picture in your readers' minds.

Similes – using 'like' –	fingernails like jagged moons
Similes – using 'as' –	as soft as lamb's wool
Personification –	the trees stooped
Metaphor –	my steel stare...

How to polish your poems

When you've finished writing a poem, reread it and look for places where you could improve it. Check whether you have used:

- powerful verbs – 'dashed' rather than 'went'

- descriptive words – 'the fox' becomes 'the slim fox'.

- poetic techniques – 'the slim fox' becomes 'the slim fox slips silently'

- too many words – 'weary' rather than 'tired, weary and exhausted'

Now show your poem to someone else to see what they think of it.

Glossary

alliteration A few words that begin with the same sound, e.g. two tiny tigers told a turtle to tickle its toes.

calligram A picture poem made of letters that show the meaning of the poem.

concrete poem A shape poem where the arrangement of the words adds to the meaning.

haiku A short type of Japanese poem – usually three lines long – that captures a moment.

kenning A type of riddle that describes something in two words linked by a hyphen.

metaphor A special poetic effect that transforms something into something else.

monologue A poem for one speaker.

personification A special poetic effect that describes things as if they are alive.

rhyme A rhyme happens when words share the same end sound pattern, e.g. cog, dog, fog, log.

rhyming couplets Pairs of lines that rhyme.

rhythm The sounds a poem makes that give it a beat.

riddle A puzzle where the subject has to be guessed.

simile A special poetic effect that compares one thing to another by using 'like' or 'as…as'.

Index

32